PRENTICE HALL DISCOV

TROUBLE AHEAD

PEARSON

Prentice
Hall

Boston, Massachusetts
Upper Saddle River, New Jersey

ISBN 0-13-363630-5

3   V059   10

PRENTICE HALL DISCOVERIES

Trouble Ahead

Is conflict always bad?

Table of Contents

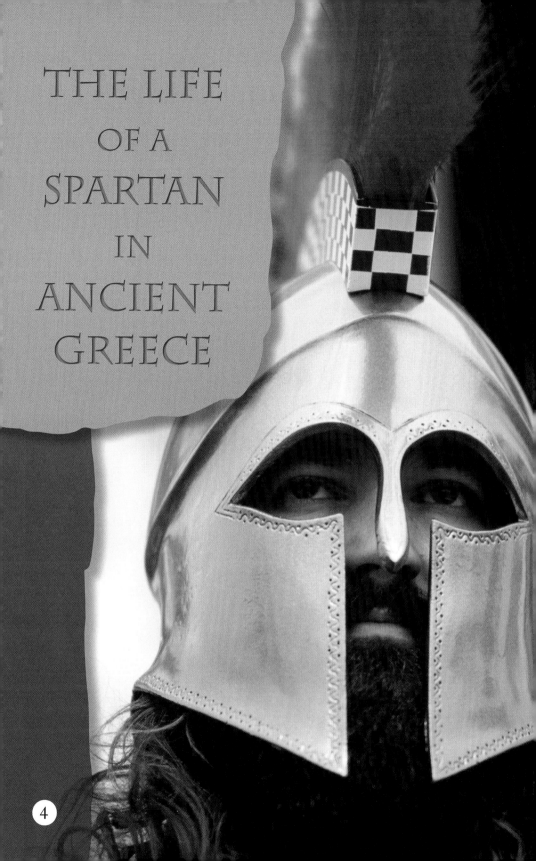

THE LIFE OF A SPARTAN IN ANCIENT GREECE

In ancient Greece, the city-state of Sparta was known for its military strength. All of its male citizens were trained to serve as soldiers. The women of Sparta were also trained to fight. In order to keep its position as the most powerful Greek city-state, Sparta was often in **conflict** with its neighbors. How did Sparta deal with conflict?

A Military City-State

Protected by mountain ranges, Sparta was located in a river valley. Although the mountains helped to keep Sparta's enemies out, the Spartans were happy to set off across those mountains in search of conquests.

One of the most famous stories that involves ancient Sparta is the legend of the Trojan War. This was a conflict between Sparta and Troy, a city whose ruins are in modern-day Turkey.

VOCABULARY

conflict (KAHN flikt) *n.* state of disagreement or argument between people, groups, or countries

This actor is dressed in an ancient Spartan military costume.

Scholars argue about the facts of the Trojan War. However, tales indicate that the Trojan War happened about 1200 B.C. It began when Helen, the Queen of Sparta, ran away with Paris, a prince of Troy. Helen and Paris's actions would **affect** the lives of many people. After ten years of war, the Greeks used trickery to bring the war to an end. They pretended to withdraw their forces at the gates of Troy, but left behind a huge wooden horse filled with warriors. The Trojans, celebrating their victory, moved the horse inside the gates. The Greek soldiers then escaped from the horse and opened the gates to admit their comrades. In this way, Greece was able to **accomplish** its defeat of Troy.

Celebrating Trojans move the large wooden horse into the city of Troy.

The Rise of Sparta

Over the years, Sparta's power grew. In 640 B.C., the Messenians, people whom the Spartans had conquered, decided to revolt. They almost defeated the Spartans. After that, a Spartan man named Lycurgus helped to strengthen Sparta's government. It became a military government, one that excelled at crushing its enemies.

Sparta's Government Ancient Greece was made up of many independent city-states. A city-state included the city and the land it controlled. Sparta became the most powerful city-state in all of Greece.

Map of ancient Greece

VOCABULARY

affect (uh FEKT) *v.* do something that produces an effect or change in someone or something

accomplish (uh KAHM plish) *v.* to succeed in doing something, especially after trying very hard

7

Sparta had an unusual government. It included a council made up of 2 kings and 28 nobles, 5 overseers, and an Assembly of male citizens. Sparta's two kings were descended from two great houses of early Sparta. The kings acted as generals in the military. They also had some religious duties. The nobles were elected for life. The council members worked together to **establish** the laws Sparta needed.

The members of the Assembly, or Spartiate, could approve or veto the council's decisions. The overseers, called the Ephorate, could veto anything approved by the council *or* the Spartiate. Thus, these five men had the most powerful roles in the government.

The Values of Sparta Spartans were taught to **dedicate** themselves to the state. They learned to **appreciate** courage, strength, and a simple life. Spartans followed rules and believed in an orderly life. They were able to get by with very little, owning few possessions. Citizens were not allowed to own silver or

Statue of Artemis, patron goddess of Sparta

gold. They also ate plain foods. In addition, Spartans believed in using as few words as possible when speaking.

Like people in the rest of Greece, Spartans worshipped many gods. The patron goddess of Sparta was Artemis. She was the goddess of hunting and wild animals. Aries, the god of war, was Sparta's patron god.

Sparta's People

Sparta had three main classes of people. Each class was **identifiable** by the occupations of its members. Those in the highest class, with the most rights, were the Spartiate. These people were related to Sparta's first settlers. The middle class of people was called the perioeci. Their ancestors had come from places that Sparta had conquered. Although they were free, the perioeci were not Spartan citizens. The people who formed the lowest class of Spartans were the helots. Helots were treated harshly, almost like slaves. Their ancestors were the Messenians, who had rebelled and did not **consent** to Spartan rule. Clashes between helots and the Spartiate were common.

VOCABULARY

establish (uh STAB lish) v. make sure of; determine

dedicate (DED i kayt) v. set apart seriously for a special purpose; devote to some work or duty

appreciate (uh PREE shee ayt) v. to understand or enjoy the good qualities or value of someone or something

identifiable (eye DEN tuh FY uh buhl) adj. recognizable; able to be identified

consent (kuhn SENT) v. agree to

The Spartiate Only Spartiate men could become citizens and have the right to vote. Both Spartiate men and women could own land. However, Spartiate men had little time to take care of their land. They were required to serve in the military from the ages of 20 to 60. One reason for this was that Sparta had acquired so many subjects through conquest. The Spartans needed to **enforce** order through their military.

The Perioeci As the middle class, the perioeci were not citizens and could not vote. However, they were expected to pay taxes. They had a great deal of freedom, even if they had no say in their government. Unlike the Spartiate, the perioeci had many career choices. They could be farmers or business people who bought, sold, or traded goods. Or they might make crafts such as pottery or other objects. Although they had to obey the Spartiate, the perioeci experienced less strife with the upper class than did the helots.

A gold cup made by Spartan craftsmen

The Helots Helots, members of the lowest class of people in Sparta, farmed the land owned by Spartiates. They were forced to give half of what they grew to their landowners. Although the helots could not be sold like slaves, they **endured** a very hard life.

The laws were not kind to helots. When helots committed a crime, there was very little they could do to **defend** their actions. They were punished much more harshly than Spartiates who committed the same crimes. In addition, the Spartiates were legally allowed to kill helots once a year. They killed those they thought might rebel against them.

Spartan Children

As soon as Spartiate babies were born, wine was poured over them to see if they were strong. It was the Greek custom to **expose** sickly children to the environment. A child who seemed weak or unhealthy was left alone in the mountains to die. In other parts of Greece, the decision to **abandon** children was left to the parents. In Sparta, government officials made the decision.

VOCABULARY

enforce (en FOHRS) *v.* make people obey a rule or law

endured (en DOORD) *v.* suffered through

defend (dee FEND) *v.* use arguments to protect someone or something from criticism; to prove that something is right

expose (ek SPOHZ) *v.* put or leave out in an unprotected place

abandon (uh BAN duhn) *v.* leave someone, especially someone you are responsible for; to go away from a place or vehicle permanently

Healthy babies were raised by strict nurses, rather than by the children's mothers. The nurses were trained to **supervise** the children's lives. The children of Spartiates were raised to be strong and healthy. Their lives were focused on physical education. However, they also learned music, song, and dance for religious events. The children's education prepared them for lives that served Sparta.

Boys At the age of seven, boys came under control of the state. They were sent away to school to live with other boys the same age. There, boys learned how to read, write, and dance. These skills were used in military life and for religious events. The main focus of a boy's education was on **survival**. At school, boys were not given much food and learned to **survive** by stealing. They also had one cloak to wear and did not use shoes. They slept on the ground. Boys were forced to compete in athletic events. They also had to fight in **battle**. As part of their training, boys were sent out at night to practice fighting the helots. Boys remained in school until the age of 20, when they became soldiers. Their strict education did not allow for independent points of view.

VOCABULARY

supervise (SOO puhr VYZ) *v.* oversee, direct, or manage work, workers, or a project

survival (suhr VY vuhl) *n.* the state of continuing to live or exist

survive (suhr VYV) *v.* continue to exist in spite of many difficulties and dangers

battle (BAT uhl) *n.* a fight between opposing armies or groups

Statue of a Spartan soldier

Girls Unlike girls in other parts of ancient Greece, Spartiate girls learned to read and write. Most girls in ancient Greece learned only household skills, such as weaving. However, helots performed these tasks for Spartiate girls. Like the boys, Spartiate girls learned how to fight in battle and learned the skills for survival. They also took part in athletic events, such as racing and throwing heavy disks. They were taught to throw javelins, long pieces of wood with pointed ends. Spartan girls stayed in shape so that when they were older, it would be **possible** for them to have healthy children.

An athlete arriving at the Olympic Games

Spartan Adults

The marriage ceremony between Spartan adults was anything but romantic. A Spartan man would take away his bride by force during the night. The bride's head would be shaved. She was also forced to wear men's clothing. After the ceremony, the husband would return to his military barracks.

Spartans could have more than one wife or husband. Husbands and wives spent very little time together. This was because the men lived their lives in the military. The main purpose of marriage was to have healthy, strong children who could protect and serve Sparta.

Adults were expected to remain in good physical condition. It would be rare to **encounter** a Spartan who was not physically fit. The people of Sparta often won first place in many Olympic events. In fact, they often won first place in more than half of the Olympic events.

Laurel wreaths were presented to the winners in early Olympic Games.

A battle scene between the Thessalians and the heavily armed Spartans. The inset shows the full battle dress of a Spartan soldier.

Men Men's lives were dedicated to Sparta until the age of 60. At age 20, after thirteen years of school, Spartan men became soldiers and lived together in barracks. When the battle cry sounded, they would **accompany** each other into battle.

After becoming soldiers, Spartan men had to **obtain** entrance into a military dining club. Each dining club ate all meals together. Members were expected to donate food each month to the club. Soldiers had to be elected into the club. If a soldier was **declined** membership, others looked down upon him.

Once in the military, men were allowed to marry. However, they could not live with their families. By age 30, Spartan men were granted citizenship. As citizens, they could attend meetings of the Assembly and vote. They could lose their citizenship if they were not brave in battle or could not pay their military dining bills.

Well trained for battle, Spartans were expert fighters. Soldiers knew how to **respond** to danger with their weapons. They were taught to overpower and **injure** their enemies. Spartans were known for fighting closely together, which made it hard for enemies to break through their battle lines. During battle, only one king would act as general. This way, only one king's life was risked at a time.

Only after the age of 60 were Spartan men able to **seek** other jobs. After that time, they might work in the government or as teachers.

Vocabulary

accompany (uh KUM puh nee) *v.* go or be together with

obtain (uhb TAYN) *v.* get something that you want, especially through your own effort, skill, or work

declined (dee KLYND) *v.* refused

respond (ri SPAHND) *v.* react to something that has been said or done

injure (IN juhr) *v.* hurt someone or yourself

seek (SEEK) *v.* try to find; search for; look for

Women After a girl married, she was considered a woman. Girls had to be at least 18 years old to be married. After marriage, Spartiate women were expected to have strong, healthy children that would one day become brave soldiers and healthy mothers. If a woman's husband was away for too long, she could marry another husband.

A bronze statue of a Spartan girl running

Spartan women had more freedom than other women of ancient Greece. In most city-states, upper-class Greek women had to spend their lives inside their homes. It was the custom to **isolate** women from the rest of the world. However, Spartan women were free to move about. Like Spartan men, the women took part in athletic events. They were expected to protect the land while their husbands were away. If necessary, they fought invaders and any helots who tried to revolt. Some Spartiate women owned their own land. This was unusual for Greek women.

The Fall of Sparta

Sparta's leaders eventually faced a **challenge**. They realized that their city-state could not fight everyone. To cut down on warfare, Sparta presented a plan to its neighbors. It offered to let other city-states ally with Sparta if they would agree to join forces to battle strong enemies. In exchange, Sparta would allow them to remain free and independent city-states. Sparta had found a new way to **resolve** conflict with its neighbors.

However, even the strongest of cities fall. Over time, Sparta slowly lost power. Invaders destroyed the city in A.D. 396. The power of Sparta was no more.

VOCABULARY

isolate (EYE suh LAYT) *v.* set apart from others; place alone

challenge (CHAL unj) *n.* something that tests strength, skill, or ability

resolve (ri ZAHLV) *v.* find a satisfactory way of dealing with a problem or difficulty; settle

Discussion Questions

1. Why do you think Sparta was in conflict with its neighbors?

2. Why might the ancient Spartans have been so focused on military force as a way to resolve disputes?

3. Do you think that force resolves conflict or creates more? Explain why.

This picture shows part of the ruins of the ancient city of Sparta.

VERSUS | Competition in Ecosystems

Have you ever tried out for a sports team? Or taken a test to find out how well you can read as compared to your classmates? Has your brother ever gotten to the last cookie before you? One way or another, you have all **encountered** competition. It's part of daily life. You also know that **conflict** is sometimes caused by competition, and sometimes it's the other way around. Competition can be a way of dealing with conflict. In nature it works both ways, too. However, in nature and certain ecosystems, competition can mean living or dying!

VOCABULARY

encounter (en KOWN tuhr) *v.* meet unexpectedly; come upon
conflict (KAHN flikt) *n.* state of disagreement or argument between people, groups, or countries

Understanding Ecosystems

Imagine a polar bear and a grizzly bear. They are two different kinds, or species, of bears. Which would win in a battle of strength? All we can do is guess. Why? These animals never encounter each other in the natural world. A polar bear lives in the Arctic tundra. Grizzly bears live in the forests of North America, Asia, and Europe. Their communities are completely different.

Take a minute to think about your community. What is it like? When you think about it, your community is not just made of people. It's made of places and things, too. Scientists use the word *ecosystem* to describe this. Ecosystems are communities of living and nonliving things that work together.

Ecosystems come in all sizes. They can be as large as an African savanna. They can also be as small as the underside of a rock. There are ecosystems within ecosystems within ecosystems.

Ecosystems can be big and small.

Every living thing in an ecosystem has a special job or role that it fills. Scientists call this role a *niche*. A niche involves everything that a living thing does to **survive** in its ecosystem. A niche includes **details** like where and what a species eats. What a species does for its community is also part of a niche. A polar bear's niche, and survival, includes the **consumption** of seals. If it didn't eat seals, then the number of seals would be too high. So, there wouldn't be enough fish to feed all of the seals. Some seals would starve. You can imagine how important every species' niche is in an ecosystem.

Giraffes and deer both have very similar niches. But they live in different ecosystems. They don't compete.

VOCABULARY

survive (suhr VYV) *v.* continue to exist in spite of many difficulties and dangers

detail (DEE tayl) *n.* a piece of information

consumption (kuhn SUMP shuhn) *n.* eating; drinking; using up

Fighting for Food and Water

Conflict occurs when species have the same or similar niches. You can **infer** that species with similar niches have similar needs. All species need resources like food, water, shelter, space to live in, and the ability to reproduce. However, the kind and amount of resources they need depends on a living thing's species and niche. This is why when a living thing is of the same species as another or shares its niche, conflict occurs. Plants, animals, and other living things don't have the ability to **negotiate** like humans do. So the way for plants and animals to **resolve** conflict is through competition.

Fierce Creatures The African savanna is a good ecosystem in which to observe competition for food. The grassland is perfect for large herds of plant-eating animals. Wildebeest, gazelles, and zebra are some of these animals. Guess what eats large plant-eating animals? Other large meat-eating animals. Big cats like lions and leopards live here. Jackals and wild dogs live here, too.

You can imagine what happens when you have several large carnivores competing for food. There will be some ferocious fights. Lions and leopards are two of these fighters. They **instinctively** compete against each other. When fighting

over fresh kills, they try to **injure** one another with sharp teeth and claws. Lions try to steal meals from leopards. Leopards steal food from lions, too.

Jackals and wild dogs hunt in packs for the large herd animals. They are smaller than the large cats. So, they **assist** each other in hunting. First, they **locate** a weak animal in a herd. Then, they **isolate** it from the rest of the animals. That's when they bring the large animal down. The sight and sound of the **thrashing** animal might attract lions. Lions steal food from jackals, but jackals also steal food from lions.

VOCABULARY

infer (in FER) *v.* assume something based on facts

negotiate (ni GOH shee ayt) *v.* discuss something in order to reach an agreement

resolve (ri ZAHLV) *v.* find a satisfactory way of dealing with a problem or difficulty; settle

instinctively (in STINGK tiv lee) *adv.* done automatically, without thinking

injure (IN juhr) *v.* hurt someone or yourself

assist (uh SIST) *v.* give help to

locate (LOH kayt) *v.* find the exact position of someone or something

isolate (EYE suh LAYT) *v.* set apart from others; place alone

thrashing (THRASH ing) *adj.* wildly moving

A female lion hunts antelopes in a national park in Botswana, Africa.

27

The carnivores of the savanna are an extreme example of competition. Many other kinds of species never actually fight. They use threatening movement and stares to scare off other animals. They don't want to get injured. Getting hurt won't help them survive.

Two dung beetles roll a ball of dung in South Africa.

Nature's Recyclers Competition for food doesn't only occur among large meat-eating animals. Insects need to eat, too. One of these insects is a dung beetle. Dung beetles live on every continent except Antarctica. Can you guess what a dung beetle's favorite food is? Dung! Dung is another word for manure or scat. Though it may smell **offensive**, this beetle's ecosystem depends on its taste for scat to keep the soil healthy. The beetle buries the scat in the ground. The scat has nutrients that help plants to grow.

Dung beetles actually compete for dung. Scientists who **monitor** the beetles have observed horn-like structures on their heads. They use them as weapons to keep other beetles away from their food. They also bury the dung so other beetles can't get to it.

Sun Worshippers Animals aren't the only living things that compete for food. Plants do, too. Plants make food from sunlight. They compete for light. Take a giant sequoia tree, for example. A giant sequoia is the largest species of tree on Earth, but it has to fight to get so large!

A giant sequoia tree starts out as a seed the size of a flake of oatmeal. Once in the ground, it takes five to seven hundred years for it to grow to its greatest height.

The largest tree on Earth is 275 feet tall.

VOCABULARY

offensive (uh FEN siv) *adj.* unpleasant

monitor (MAHN i tuhr) *v.* carefully watch, listen to, or examine something over a period of time

Other trees **affect** its chance of survival. They may create too much shade on the forest floor. A young giant sequoia can starve from lack of light.

Some giant sequoias find a way to live even with all of the shade. They **respond** to available light by growing toward it. That's why you see trees that lean to one side. They look like they are falling over, but they are actually quite healthy. Also, each mature giant sequoia tree produces thousands of seeds. This way, some seeds are sure to survive and grow into mature trees.

Desert Dwellers Water is another resource needed by living things to survive. Over one-fifth of Earth's land is desert. Deserts are dry and hot. They receive less than 10 inches of rain a year. Water is in high demand and creates competition.

There is a lizard that lives in the Australian desert. It is called a thorny devil. It is **identifiable** by savage-looking spines that cover its entire body. About the size of a human hand, it looks mean, but it's not. Its life consists of eating ants and finding enough water to live.

A thorny devil's whole body is designed to catch water. When it rains, the water hitting its body doesn't flow off onto the ground. Instead, its spines direct the water right into its mouth! Also, if you **examine** their skin, there are thousands of tiny grooves along their legs and backs. If they are standing in a puddle, these grooves soak up the water and direct it to their mouth.

Vocabulary

affect (uh FEKT) *v.* do something that produces an effect or change in someone or something

respond (ri SPAHND) *v.* react to something that has been said or done

identifiable (eye DEN tuh FY uh buhl) *adj.* recognizable; able to be identified

examine (eg ZAM uhn) *v.* look at carefully

Thorny devils in the Australian desert. It is one of many animals that compete for water.

31

The creosote bush also lives in a desert ecosystem. Its roots go deep into the ground. They stretch out in all directions. If any other seed falls near the plant, it won't survive because the creosote's roots gather all of the water in the area. The creosote bush also has a secret weapon. It **exudes** a special chemical into the ground. The chemical is like a poison to most other plants. Very few plants can grow near creosote bushes.

Fighting for a Place to Live

Shelter and space to live are also resources necessary to the survival of a species. Living things may die if there is not enough shelter to hide from enemies and bad weather. Also, every species needs enough room to fill its niche. If an ecosystem is too crowded or gets smaller, a living thing may not be able to do its job.

Space Savers Most people have heard of rain forests. The loss of these ecosystems is an **issue** that many people discuss. Scientists believe that more than half of the world's species live in rain forests. This means that competition for space is intense!

An air plant, or epiphyte, is one that deals with **opposition** creatively. This plant doesn't even try to compete for space on the ground. It grows on other very tall plants, like trees. How does this work? Wind or birds drop an air plant's seeds high up on the other plants. The air plant's roots anchor it to the tree. The air plant doesn't need soil for nutrients and water. It gets those things from dust in the air and rain. A bromeliad is one kind of air plant. It is a small ecosystem in itself. The strangler fig is

A bromeliad is an ecosystem in itself.

another air plant. The fig **systematically** wraps its roots around the plant it lives on. The plant strangles from too little air and light, and dies.

VOCABULARY

exude (eg ZYOOD) *v.* give off; ooze

issue (ISH oo) *n.* problem or subject that people discuss

opposition (ahp uh ZISH uhn) *n.* strong disagreement with; protest against

systematically (sis tuh MAT ik lee) *adv.* orderly

Underwater Warriors A coral reef, like the rain forest, is home to some of the most diverse creatures on Earth. It may seem like it is a peaceful place, but it's not! Found in the ocean, corals need a certain amount of space to live. They'll fight other corals for space. Some kinds of corals have long arm-like tentacles. These tentacles sting other corals. Sometimes the sting is so powerful, it **ravages** a competing coral and the competitor dies.

Some corals also produce a substance in their stomachs that "eats" other corals. It's the same kind of substance that breaks down food. Corals also have another weapon. They release a kind of poison into the water. This injures neighboring corals. The aggressive coral grows taller than the injured corals. The injured corals don't get enough light and die.

Fighting to Reproduce

Every species must reproduce or it will die out. Animals find other animals to mate with. Plants spread their seeds and pollen. Competition for mates, seed spreaders, and pollinators can take some interesting forms.

Fancy Feathers Though some birds fight, other birds use a more creative approach to compete for mates. Male nightingales sing to attract a mate. Other male nightingales **challenge** the singer by interrupting his song with their own songs. This is done to impress the females. If a male is lucky, his song will attract a female nightingale.

This Emperor of Germany's bird of paradise competes with other males to attract a female.

A bird of paradise has very showy feathers. A male will perform elaborate dances to attract a female. It **exposes** its feathers by spreading its wings out and arching its back. It will actually freeze in this pose when females approach.

VOCABULARY

ravage (RAV ij) *v.* violently destroy; ruin

challenge (CHAL unj) *v.* test strength, skill, or ability

expose (ek SPOHZ) *v.* put or leave out in an unprotected place

Winners and Losers

Competition in an ecosystem impacts the creatures that live there. One species is left to fill the niche, but what happens to the losing species varies. Some are able to adapt. They develop new skills and behavior that allow them to live in the same ecosystem. The pitcher plant is an example. It makes its food from sunlight. Sometimes the soil where it grows doesn't provide enough nutrients, so it also depends on its consumption of insects!

The last male passenger pigeon died in 1912.

Other species are forced to leave their ecosystem as a result of competition. They may or may not survive. The hermit warbler is an example of this. This small songbird normally lives in western North America, but it is being pushed out of its ecosystem by the Townsend's warbler. The Townsend's warbler is much more aggressive. Scientists worry that the hermit warbler will become extinct.

Often, the final result of competition is death. Take the case of the passenger pigeon. At one time, there were billions of passenger pigeons in the world. Branches broke when huge groups of them landed on trees. It seemed there were as many pigeons as there were insects. They lived in forests, but humans cut down the trees for homes. The birds started eating farmers' crops and people shot them. Other people hunted them. In 1879, one billion birds were captured in Michigan! The last bird died in a zoo in 1914. Today, the passenger pigeon is extinct.

The Balance of Nature

Sometimes in an ecosystem, there are fewer resources to go around. Plants and animals sharing similar niches are forced to compete. They compete for water, food, shelter, space to live, and even mates for reproduction. The "winners" are able to keep filling the same niche. The "losers" must adapt or move on. Under the worst circumstances, the losers simply die out.

We help other species every time we put one of these items into a recycling bin and not the garbage.

Today, the number one cause of extinction is the loss of habitat. This means that a species loses its shelter and space to live in. Sadly, human activity has caused this to happen. Trees are cut down so homes and businesses can be built. Large areas of land are cleared so food can be grown. Our niche has placed us in direct competition and conflict with many other species. Yet, we, as a species, are adaptable. It's the other species that lose.

What can humans do to help? Take action by using fewer resources, for starters. Recycle things like paper and food containers. Take shorter showers and make sure to turn off the water when it's not in use. Watch the news and keep informed about our environment. Our actions can make all the difference!

Discussion Questions

1. Think about the ways in which humans compete for a limited resource, such as oil. In what ways might this competition cause conflict? How might we, as humans, try to resolve it?

2. Think about competition in plant and animal eco-systems. In what ways might a competition between two species of animal cause a conflict? How might those animals resolve it?

3. Do you think competition causes conflict? Or, do you think it is a result of conflict? Explain your answer.

THE IDITAROD
The Last Great Race on Earth

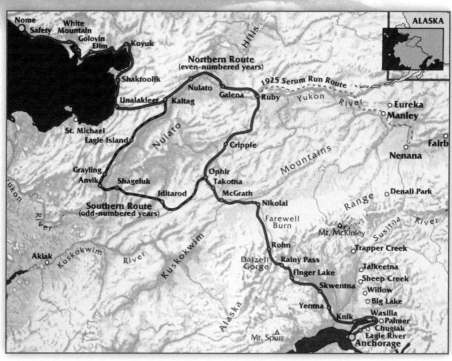

This map shows the Iditarod trail and the race checkpoints along the way. The race alternates routes every year. The northern route is used in even-numbered years and the southern route is used in odd-numbered years.

It's early March 2007, and 82 dogsled racers—known as mushers—are gathered at the starting line in Anchorage, Alaska. With them in the snowy, freezing weather are about 1,000 dogs. Together, the dogs and humans will **compete** in what some consider the most difficult race on Earth—the Iditarod Sled Dog Race.

The Iditarod, a race that covers over 1,000 miles, is grueling. But the distance is not the only thing that makes it so hard. The real **challenge** comes from the course itself, an unending stretch of cold, snowy, isolated, unpredictable Alaskan wilderness. Mushers are in a constant battle with the elements just to finish this incredible race.

Those who do **survive** and finish say there is nothing like it. The feeling of conquering both nature and human limits is glorious. That is why many mushers come back, year after year, to try their luck in crossing the unforgiving Alaskan terrain.

VOCABULARY

compete (kuhm PEET) v. try to gain something; be better or more successful than someone else

challenge (CHAL unj) n. something that tests strength, skill, or ability

survive (suhr VYV) v. continue to exist in spite of many difficulties and dangers

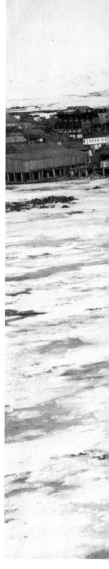

Nome, Alaska, in the early 20th century

A Race to Save Lives

The origin of the Iditarod goes back over 100 years, to the early 1900s. That is when gold was first discovered in the area around Nome, Alaska. The lure of gold brought thousands of people to Alaska. Towns like Nome and Iditarod grew rapidly.

The miners in these places needed a way to transport gold, mail, and supplies during the winter months when ships couldn't reach the harbor. So, they turned to dogsleds. Soon, dogsled trails **traversed** this remote area.

By 1920, the gold rush was over. People **abandoned** the town of Iditarod. Eventually, it was almost deserted. However, sled dogs still continued to use the trails that led to Nome, delivering mail and other important supplies during the cold winter months.

Then, in January of 1925, tragedy struck Nome. Two Native Alaskan children died of an infectious disease called diphtheria. Diphtheria is very contagious. The doctor in Nome was worried. His hospital didn't have the medicine he needed to fight the disease. Without it, hundreds of people would certainly die. The townspeople prayed that the doctor would **locate** some medicine and have it delivered quickly.

Gunnar Kaasen and his dog team arrive in Nome
carrying medicine on March 18, 1925.

VOCABULARY

traversed (truh VERST) *v.* went across

abandon (uh BAN duhn) *v.* leave someone, especially someone
you are responsible for; to go away from a place or vehicle
permanently

locate (LOH kayt) *v.* find the exact position of someone or
something

The problem was that nothing arrived quickly in Nome during January. Nome residents **relied** on a delivery system that used both a train and dogsleds. It took months for mail and supplies to arrive. Nome often received only two mail deliveries all winter.

Desperate to save lives, the doctor **appealed** to Alaskan officials. Together they hatched a plan. Teams of dogsled racers would relay the diphtheria serum to Nome. The relay could take up to two weeks, depending on the weather, but it was the best anyone could do. It would have to work.

The serum was first transported by train from Anchorage to Nenana. Then, on January 27, twenty mushers and their dogs got ready to rush the medicine the next 674 miles to Nome.

Leonhard Seppala with two of his sled dogs

This statue of Balto stands in New York's Central Park.

The mushers were stationed at intervals along the trail. One musher would complete his leg of the relay. Then he would hand off the serum to the next musher, who would set out into the cold, snowy wilderness.

The weather was worse than anyone had expected. The mushers **endured** numbing cold, strong winds, and storms. Through it all, they had to be careful that the medicine didn't freeze.

With their determination, the mushers **accomplished** the impossible. They got the serum to Nome in less than six days. The mushers became national heroes.

Particularly impressive was Leonhard Seppala, who, together with his lead dog, Togo, covered over 260 miles of the trail. Togo would share the spotlight with Balto, Gunnar Kaasen's lead dog. Kaasen was the musher who traveled the final leg of the journey and brought the medicine into Nome. Balto became famous. Today, there is a statue of him in Central Park in New York City.

VOCABULARY

rely (ree LY) *v.* trust someone or something to do what you need or expect them to do

appeal (uh PEEL) *v.* make an urgent request for

endured (en DOORD) *v.* suffered through

accomplish (uh KAHM plish) *v.* to succeed in doing something, especially after trying very hard

The Beginning of a Tradition

Though the mushers and their race to save lives became famous, the Iditarod trail eventually fell into disuse. Planes and snowmobiles made dogsleds unnecessary. By the mid 1900s, traveling by dogsled was considered old-fashioned.

Then, in 1967, a celebration was organized for Alaska's centennial year. It was the hundredth anniversary of Alaska's purchase from Russia. Looking for ways to celebrate, organizers decided on a dogsled race. They would recreate part of the historic relay that had saved so many lives in 1925.

At first, recreating the race didn't seem **possible**. People said it couldn't be done. But after a lot of hard work, 58 mushers raced for 2 days and 56 miles.

A second race was held in 1969. Then, in 1973, the official Iditarod Sled Dog Race, with its 1,000-mile plus route, was established. Every year since then, the conflict between humans and nature has been waged in the Alaskan wilderness.

The Jr. Iditarod

Iditarod race rules **restrict** entrance to those under the age of 18. So what's a young dogsled racer to do?

Fortunately, since 1978, mushers between the ages of 14 and 17 have had their own Iditarod race. Held on the

Dusten Regars runs his team down the trail during the 2006 Jr. Iditarod.

weekend before the big race starts, the 160-mile Jr. Iditarod attracts young mushers from all over. Not surprisingly, many of them are the children of Iditarod racers.

For two days, these young mushers travel over snowy trails. They spend the night around a campfire, and they talk with one another while the dogs are **gnawing** on bones. The winners are awarded scholarships, but for most of these teens, just being in the race is its own reward.

Vocabulary

possible (PAHS uh buhl) *adj.* able to be done

restrict (ri STRIKT) *v.* keep within certain limits; put certain limitations on

gnawing (NAW ing) *v.* biting and cutting with teeth

Ready, Set, Mush!

It's race day, 2007. The mushers and their teams are waiting at the starting line in Anchorage. Each musher wears a number. The racers will start the race in the order of their numbers, from lowest to highest.

Lance Mackey has number 13. Most people consider 13 to be an unlucky number, but you won't **convince** Mackey of that. It's the number his father, Dick, and his brother, Rick, both wore when each finally won the Iditarod.

Something else gives Mackey confidence as well. This is his sixth Iditarod. Both his father and his brother won the race on their sixth tries. He hopes to keep that tradition alive.

The odds are certainly stacked against Mackey. A few years ago, he was diagnosed with cancer. The treatment he had still makes it hard for him to swallow, which means he won't be able to eat much on the trail. That could leave him too weak to finish. Some people think he's crazy to even attempt this race.

There's another reason people aren't giving him much of a chance. Just a few weeks ago, Mackey won Alaska's other big dogsled race, the Yukon Quest. Now everyone thinks he and his dogs must be too tired to really compete.

This picture shows Lance Mackey and his team as they approach Nome.

Lance Mackey and his dogs arrive at the end of the race.

Lance won't let all the talk **affect** him. He has never **hesitated** in his quest to win the Iditarod. Now, he feels that this is his year. He sets out to prove it. Two days after the race begins, he grabs the lead. It won't be that easy, though. Soon other mushers overtake him and beat him to the next checkpoints. Severe frostbite in his finger slows him down.

Still, Lance pushes ahead. He knows he can do it. He trusts his dogs. There's Larry, the brains of his team, and Fudge, his dependable lead dog. Together they move on, traveling through brutal winds and temperatures of minus fifty degrees Fahrenheit.

Finally, just over nine days after he set out, Lance Mackey arrives in Nome. He has won the Iditarod! More importantly, he has done something no one else has ever done before, something people claimed was impossible. He has won Alaska's two biggest dogsled races in the same year.

VOCABULARY

affect (uh FEKT) *v.* do something that produces an effect or change in someone or something

hesitated (HEZ i tayt id) *v.* stopped because of indecision

50

Lance Mackey, the 2007 Iditarod Champion, with two of his dogs.

It Must Be Love

Why do people race in the Iditarod? As the racers themselves point out, it's not for the money. It costs more to run the race than the winners get in prize money. There are dogs to train and there is equipment to buy and transportation to pay for. Every racer has to ship food for 16 or more dogs to each race checkpoint.

For most racers, competing in the Iditarod is a family affair. Family members help the racers pack and ship food before the race. They often meet racers at checkpoints along the way or wait for them at the finish line in Nome.

For many families, the Iditarod is an annual ritual. Racers compete in the Iditarod over and over again. Some have already won it and are looking for more victories. Others still **seek** that elusive first win.

It's All About the Dogs

For most Iditarod mushers, how well they race really depends on their dogs. Most Iditarod racers use Alaskan huskies as their sled dogs. Many racers own their own kennels. They raise and train their sled dogs, spending many hours with them and teaching them commands. Here is a look at who's who on a sled dog team.

The Lead Dog The lead dog is the dog at the front of the team. Lead dogs must be smart. They have to follow the trail and **instinctively respond** to the musher's commands. The rest of the dogs are hitched up in pairs behind the lead dog.

Mark Moderow and his team during the 2004 Iditarod

The Swing Dogs The job of the swing dogs is to keep the team on the trail when the sled turns. This can be hard if the turn is sharp or the trail is steep. Without good swing dogs, the sled is more **liable** to overturn.

The Team Dogs These are the real pullers on the team. Their strength keeps the sled moving. Most team dogs aren't **coaxed** into pulling and running. They just love to do it naturally.

The Wheel Dogs These dogs are hitched directly in front of the sled and help the musher steer. They also pull the sled loose if it gets stuck.

VOCABULARY

seek (SEEK) *v.* try to find; search for; look for

instinctively (in STINGK tiv lee) *adv.* done automatically, without thinking

respond (ri SPAHND) *v.* react to something that has been said or done

liable (LY uh buhl) *adj.* likely to do something or to happen

coaxed (KOHKST) *v.* persuaded by gentle urging

Famous Racers

There have been many famous Iditarod racers over the years. Here is a look at some of them.

Rick Swensen Rick Swensen won his first Iditarod in 1977. Since then, he has gone on to win the race four more times, for a total of five victories. He has won the Iditarod more times than any other racer. He is also the only racer to win the Iditarod in three different decades—the 1970s, the 1980s, and the 1990s.

Susan Butcher Susan Butcher won the Iditarod four times, one less than Rick Swensen. She is also the woman with the most Iditarod victories. Butcher might have won it five times, but she had to drop out of the race one year when her team **encountered** a moose. The moose **mauled** several of her dogs, killing one of them.

Martin Buser Martin Buser has also won the Iditarod four times. However, he is most famous for clocking the fastest race time ever. Iditarod winners usually take about nine days to complete the course. Martin managed to do it in eight days and 22 hours, the only racer ever to do so.

Gary Paulsen Gary Paulsen is famous not as an Iditarod winner but as a writer. He is an avid sled dog racer and has entered the Iditarod a few times. The race has made its way into more than one of his books. Gary says you can talk about the race and train for it, but "it is not something you can do . . . . And yet you do it and then it becomes something you don't want to end—ever. You want the race, the exultation, the joy and beauty of it to go on and on. . . ."

Rachel Scdoris Rachel Scdoris is a young woman famous for being the first blind person to race in the Iditarod. Rachel had to fight hard to enter the race. In order not to be **injured**, Rachel needed an escort who could tell her about the trail. Some people thought that her escort should not be allowed. However, Rachel **pleaded** her case, and she was finally allowed to race. In her first year, 2005, she had to drop out and didn't finish. Finally, in 2006, she managed to complete the race.

VOCABULARY

encounter (en KOWN tuhr) *v.* meet unexpectedly; come upon
mauled (MAWLD) *v.* badly injured by biting and tearing
injure (IN juhr) *v.* hurt someone or yourself
plead (PLEED) *v.* beg

A Race Like No Other

From the outside, it might seem like Iditarod racers are a little crazy. After all, who would want to travel for over a week in a cold, frozen, dangerous wilderness, without much sleep or food?

The racers, of course, don't see it that way. For many of them, the Iditarod is in their blood. Sure, the racers are cold, they are hungry, and sometimes they are even tired enough to hallucinate. However, nothing beats the feeling of finishing and triumphing over the elements.

The cold, the wind, the distance, the exhaustion, and the danger are what make the Iditarod special.

The racers wouldn't have it any other way.

Discussion Questions

1. How important is the relationship between mushers and their dogs? What do mushers do for their dogs? What do dogs do for their mushers?

2. How is battling the elements part of the Iditarod's appeal? Why do people seek participation in this conflict?

3. Would you ever want to be an Iditarod racer? Why or why not?

John Barrons and his team travel down a hillside to Puntilla Lake during the 2006 Iditarod.

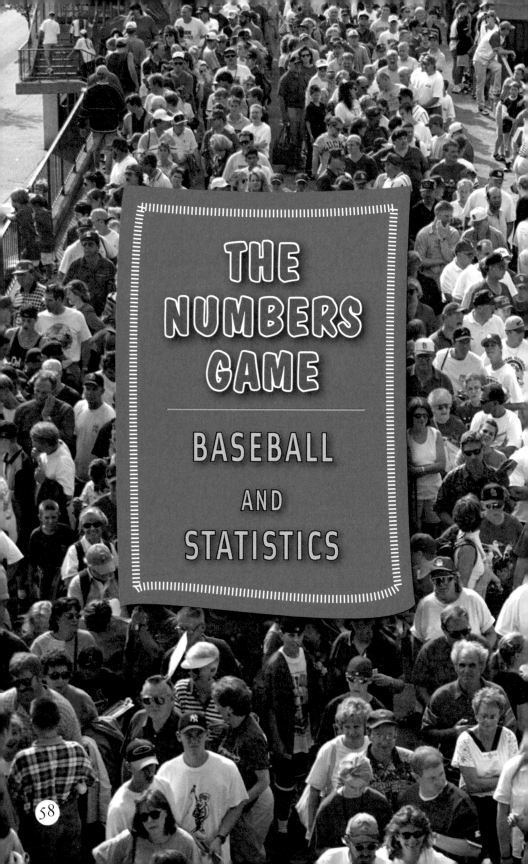

THE NUMBERS GAME

BASEBALL

AND

STATISTICS

Baseball fans can talk all day about their favorite sport. They like to **argue** about it, too! In fact, there's nothing like a "who's best" question to spark a heated discussion. Who's the best hitter? Who's the best pitcher? What's the best team? Asking one of these questions is guaranteed to start a friendly **conflict**.

The opinions start flying. Next come the numbers as each fan **responds** with the **support** of statistics to prove their point of view.

What are these statistics that baseball fans **rely** on? How are they calculated? What do they tell about a player or a team? Let's **examine** these stats. Let's see how they relate to the "who's best" questions.

VOCABULARY

argue (ahr GYOO) *v.* have a disagreement; quarrel; dispute

conflict (KAHN flikt) *n.* state of disagreement or argument between people, groups, or countries

respond (ri SPAHND) *v.* react to something that has been said or done

support (suh POHRT) *n.* evidence or reasons for

rely (ree LY) *v.* trust someone or something to do what you need or expect them to do

examine (eg ZAM uhn) *v.* look at carefully

Baseball fans wait to enter Busch Stadium in St. Louis for a game between the Chicago Cubs and the St. Louis Cardinals on August 7, 1998. The Cardinals defeated the Cubs 16 to 3.

At Bat: The Best Hitters

Let's begin with "Who's the best hitter?" After all, hits are what the **game** is all about. Getting them is good, and getting lots of them is better. That's why fans often turn to the number of hits so they can **support** their arguments about the game's best players.

Here are Major League Baseball's lifetime leaders in hits.

Player	Career Hits	At Bats	Games
Pete Rose	4,256	14,053	3,562
Ty Cobb	4,191	11,429	3,035
Hank Aaron	3,771	12,364	3,298
Stan Musial	3,630	10,972	3,026
Tris Speaker	3,514	10,195	2,789

At the top, you'll find the player with the most hits ever, the Cincinnati Reds' Pete Rose. Next is Ty Cobb, a Hall of Fame player who starred for the Detroit Tigers in the early part of the century. In third place is Hank Aaron, the great slugger of the 1950s and 1960s. He happens to hold the record for the most home runs ever, but we'll get to that later.

The answer to the question seems easily **identifiable** with a list like this. But the fans still cannot **conclude** who is the game's best hitter. "What about at bats?" someone shouts, and they're right, of course. Look at the list's second column.

Pete Rose had the most hits, but he also had the most chances. He went to the plate some 2,500 more times than Ty Cobb. Despite all those at bats, he only **obtained** a few dozen more hits.

Ty Cobb

Batting Average

Another statistic makes it **possible** to get a better sense of how a player did each time at the plate. It's batting average. This stat takes into account the number of chances a player had.

To calculate batting average (BA), divide the number of hits by the number of at bats.

$$\frac{H\ (hits)}{AB\ (at\ bats)} = BA\ (batting\ average)$$

A player with 5 hits in 10 at bats would have a batting average of .500, since 5 divided by 10 = .500.

Let's look at the BA for the top three hit makers of all time.

Pete Rose $\dfrac{4{,}256}{14{,}053} = .303$

Ty Cobb $\dfrac{4{,}191}{11{,}429} = .367$

Hank Aaron $\dfrac{3{,}771}{12{,}364} = .305$

Hank Aaron

You can imagine Ty Cobb fans **savoring** the results, shouting, ".367, 367." Rose wasn't close to Cobb, and falls a hair below Aaron. Indeed, if you **refer** to a list of players ranked by batting average, you get a very different picture of the game's top hitters.

Player	Batting Average
Ty Cobb	.367
Rogers Hornsby	.358
Ed Delahanty	.346
Tris Speaker	.345
Billy Hamilton	.344
Ted Williams	.344
Dan Brouthers	.342
Harry Heilmann	.342
Babe Ruth	.342

The Long Ball

Apparently, Ty Cobb is the hitting king. To Hank Aaron fans, however, it's not that simple. "Hold on," they say. "You're forgetting a small **detail**. Batting average isn't the only hitting stat."

VOCABULARY

savoring (SAY vuhr ing) v. enjoying; tasting with delight

refer (ri FER) v. look back

apparently (uh PER uhnt lee) adv. appearing to be true

detail (DEE tayl) n. a piece of information

Indeed, batting average doesn't tell you about the kind of hits a player gets. Each hit isn't equal. A double gets you two bases. A triple gets you three. The home run, of course, is the king of all hits. The batter, and everyone else on base, scores.

Let's **consult** a list of baseball's all-time home run kings.

Player	Home Runs
Hank Aaron	755
Barry Bonds	734
Babe Ruth	714
Willie Mays	660
Sammy Sosa	588
Frank Robinson	586
Mark McGwire	583

Right away you'll see Hank Aaron's name at the top. After **reflecting** a little longer, you may notice something else: This list has different names than the list of batting average leaders.

In general, players who smash home runs don't have the best batting averages. Players with the best averages don't stroke the most home runs. It's too great a **challenge** to do both things well.

Notice, however, the one exception—the mighty Yankee slugger Babe Ruth. Ruth is the number three home run hitter, and he is tied for sixth in batting average. Babe Ruth could do it all—even pitch—but that's another story!

Total Bases

Is Babe Ruth the best ever? Let's examine one more stat to find out. It's called SLG (slugging percentage), and it's based on total bases. For SLG, a single counts as one base. A double counts as two, a triple three, and a home run four.

VOCABULARY

consult (kuhn SULT) *v.* seek an opinion from; ask advice of

reflecting (ri FLEKT ing) *v.* thinking seriously

challenge (CHAL unj) *n.* something that tests strength, skill, or ability

Babe Ruth watches his home run go over the outfield wall at League Park in Cleveland in August, 1927.

To get the slugging percentage, you add up all the bases and divide by the number of at bats.

$$\frac{\text{TB (total bases)}}{\text{AB (at bats)}} = \text{SLG (slugging percentage)}$$

SLG sounds complicated, but it's not so hard. As an example, we'll calculate the 2006 SLG of St. Louis Cardinal Albert Pujols. In 535 at bats, he had 94 singles, 33 doubles, 1 triple, and 49 home runs, for an SLG of .671.

(94 x 1) + (33 x 2) + (1 x 3) + (49 x 4) = 359 total bases

$$\frac{359}{535} = .671$$

Below are baseball's lifetime leaders in slugging percentage.

Player	Slugging Percentage
Babe Ruth	.690
Ted Williams	.634
Lou Gehrig	.632
Jimmie Foxx	.609
Barry Bonds	.608
Hank Greenberg	.605
Manny Ramirez	.600
Todd Helton	.593

Who is at the top? Babe Ruth! It's hard to argue that this statistic should **establish** him as the greatest slugger ever. And what about Albert Pujols and his .671? Many **speculate** that Pujols will end up high on the lifetime list by the time his career is over.

On the Mound: The Best Pitchers

Hitting is only half of the game. What about pitching? Do fans argue about pitchers like they do about hitters? Absolutely. They just rely on different stats to support their arguments.

The first such stat is wins. After all, winning is the objective of the game.

Here are baseball's lifetime pitching leaders.

Player	Lifetime Wins
Cy Young	511
Walter Johnson	417
Grover Alexander	373
Christy Mathewson	373
Jim Galvin	365
Warren Spahn	363
Kid Nichols	361
Roger Clemens	348

VOCABULARY

establish (uh STAB lish) *v.* make sure of; determine

speculate (SPEK yuh LAYT) *v.* make a prediction

Cy Young is the easy winner here with nearly a hundred more victories than Walter Johnson. Young, who pitched a century ago, definitely had good stuff. In fact, the yearly award that baseball gives to top pitchers is named after him.

Cy Young

Fans **appreciate** Cy Young's win totals. Few, however, can be **coaxed** into saying that Young is the best on the basis of wins alone. "A win is out of a pitcher's control," they would argue. "A good pitcher can **lose** if his teammates don't hit and score."

It's true, and so is the opposite. A terrible pitcher can **win** if his teammates score enough runs.

Earned Run Average

Most fans **monitor** a different stat to evaluate pitchers. It's called the Earned Run Average (ERA). Lower is better with ERA. Most pitchers have an ERA of 4 or 5 for a season. Under 3 is great. Under 2 is unbelievable.

To calculate ERA, multiply the number of earned runs charged to a pitcher by 9. Then divide the result by the number of innings pitched.

$$\frac{(\text{earned runs allowed}) \times 9}{\text{IP (innings pitched)}} = \text{ERA (earned run average)}$$

VOCABULARY

appreciate (uh PREE shee ayt) *v.* to understand or enjoy the good qualities or value of someone or something

coaxed (KOHKST) *v.* persuaded by gentle urging

lose (LOOZ) *v.* not win a game, argument, or war

win (WIN) *v.* be the best or first in a competition, game, or election

monitor (MAHN i tuhr) *v.* carefully watch, listen to, or examine something over a period of time

Why multiply by 9? Because there are nine innings in a game. ERA shows how many runs a pitcher gives up per game. As an example, let's calculate the 2006 ERA for Houston Astro's ace Roger Clemens. He pitched 113.1 innings and gave up 29 earned runs.

$$\frac{(29 \times 9)}{113.1} = \frac{261}{113.1} = 2.30$$

As you can see, Clemens's ERA for 2006 was 2.30. Pretty impressive!

Here are baseball's lifetime leaders in ERA.

Player	Lifetime ERA
Ed Walsh	1.82
Addie Joss	1.89
Al Spalding	2.04
Mordecai Brown	2.06
John Ward	2.10
Christy Mathewson	2.13
Tommy Bond	2.14
Rube Waddell	2.16

As you see, Cy Young is not on the list. In fact, he doesn't even make the top 30. Does that mean Ed Walsh is the greatest pitcher ever? Nope, it means that baseball fans will just have to keep on arguing.

Playing Together: The Greatest Teams

Fans love to argue about teams, not just players. There's no conflict, however, about the most successful team in baseball history. The New York Yankees have won 26 World Series titles. That's far more than the runner-up St. Louis Cardinals' 10.

You can still get a good argument going, however, by asking "Which was the greatest team in any single season?" The simplest way to settle it is to consult the record books.

Here are the five teams that won the most regular season games.

Team	Year	W-L
Seattle Mariners	2001	116–46
Chicago Cubs	1906	116–36
New York Yankees	1998	114–48
Cleveland Indians	1954	111–43
New York Yankees	1927	110–44

Are the Seattle Mariners and the Chicago Cubs equally great since they both won 116 games? "No," shouts a Cubs fan, and the fan is correct. Baseball teams haven't always played the same number of games in a season. A team playing fewer games has fewer chances to rack up wins.

The New York Yankees celebrate winning the 1998 World Series against the San Diego Padres.

You can **adjust** for this by looking at another stat, the win-loss percentage.

To calculate it, divide the number of wins by the number of games played.

W/GP = win-loss percentage

$$\frac{\text{W (wins)}}{\text{GP (games played)}} = \text{win-loss percentage}$$

1906 Chicago Cubs	$\frac{116}{152}$ =	.763
1954 Cleveland Indians	$\frac{111}{154}$ =	.721
2001 Seattle Mariners	$\frac{116}{162}$ =	.716
1927 New York Yankees	$\frac{110}{154}$ =	.714
1998 New York Yankees	$\frac{114}{162}$ =	.704

As you can see, using win-loss percentage adjusts the rankings of these five teams. Cubs fans are happy. So are Cleveland fans. Then, from across the room, you hear a Yankee fan say, "Excuse me."

"That's all good and fine," she says, "but winning regular season games isn't the goal of a baseball team. It's winning the World Series. Why don't you **trace** the success of those five teams in the playoffs?"

VOCABULARY

adjust (uh JUST) *v.* to gradually get used to a new situation by making small changes to the way you do things
trace (TRAYS) *v.* follow the history of

73

It seems like a fair idea, and here's what you find out. The two Yankee teams each won the World Series. Both the Cubs and Indians lost in the series. The Mariners didn't even reach the series. The Yankees knocked them out.

No wonder baseball fans in other cities hate the Yankees. No matter how you look at it, New York always seems to come out on top!

Beyond the Numbers

Of course, numbers can't tell the whole story about the best players and the best teams. It's hard to measure player qualities like leadership and poise. And, as the example of the Yankees points out, not all wins, hits, and pitches are equal. What really counts is what happens in October, the month when the World Series is held.

There's also conflict about how much you can trust the accuracy of statistics. In the early days of baseball, not all statistics were recorded. Some record book numbers are reconstructed—put together later using box scores and newspaper accounts.

Still others argue that old stats are meaningless, even if they are correct. That's because for decades African American players were kept out of the major leagues.

This changed when Jackie Robinson broke the color line in 1947. Still, players like Babe Ruth and Ty Cobb earned their stats without having to face black players. If they had had to hit and pitch against *all* the best of the best, who knows how they would have done?

Discussion Questions

1. What was the most interesting fact about baseball statistics you learned while reading this chapter? Explain.

2. Do you think statistics can help settle disputes over questions like "Who is the greatest player ever?" Why or why not?

3. Who is your favorite baseball player? What do you like about him? Explain.

Jackie Robinson of the Brooklyn Dodgers slides safely into home during a game at Ebbets Field in Brooklyn, New York in 1956.

Glossary

abandon (uh BAN duhn) *v.* leave someone, especially someone you are responsible for; to go away from a place or vehicle permanently **11, 42**

accompany (uh KUM puh nee) *v.* go or be together with **16**

accomplish (uh KAHM plish) *v.* to succeed in doing something, especially after trying very hard **6, 45**

adjust (uh JUST) *v.* to gradually get used to a new situation by making small changes to the way you do things **73**

affect (uh FEKT) *v.* do something that produces an effect or change in someone or something **6, 30, 50**

apparently (uh PER uhnt lee) *adv.* appearing to be true **63**

appeal (uh PEEL) *v.* make an urgent request for **44**

appreciate (uh PREE shee ayt) *v.* to understand or enjoy the good qualities or value of someone or something **8, 69**

argue (ahr GYOO) *v.* have a disagreement; quarrel; dispute **59**

assist (uh SIST) *v.* give help to **27**

battle (BAT uhl) *n.* a fight between opposing armies or groups **12**

challenge (CHAL unj) *n.* something that tests strength, skill, or ability **19, 41, 64**

challenge (CHAL unj) *v.* test strength, skill, or ability **34**

coaxed (KOHKST) *v.* persuaded by gentle urging **53, 69**

compete (kuhm PEET) *v.* try to gain something; be better or more successful than someone else **41**

conclude (kuhn KLOOD) *v.* form an opinion **60**

conflict (KAHN flikt) *n.* state of disagreement or argument between people, groups, or countries **5, 23, 59**

consent (kuhn SENT) *v.* agree to **9**

consult (kuhn SULT) *v.* seek an opinion from; ask advice of **64**

consumption (kuhn SUMP shuhn) *n.* eating; drinking; using up **25**

convince (kuhn VINS) *v.* make someone feel certain that something is true **48**

declined (dee KLYND) *v.* refused **16**

dedicate (DED i kayt) *v.* set apart seriously for a special purpose; devote to some work or duty **8**

defend (dee FEND) *v.* use arguments to protect someone or something from criticism; to prove that something is right **11**

detail (DEE tayl) *n.* a piece of information **25, 63**

encounter (en KOWN tuhr) *v.* meet unexpectedly; come upon **15, 23, 54**

endured (en DOORD) *v.* suffered through **11, 45**

enforce (en FOHRS) *v.* make people obey a rule or law **10**

establish (uh STAB lish) *v.* make sure of; determine **8, 67**

examine (eg ZAM uhn) *v.* look at carefully **31, 59**

expose (ek SPOHZ) *v.* put or leave out in an unprotected place **11, 35**

exude (eg ZYOOD) *v.* give off; ooze **32**

game (GAYM) *n.* activity or sport in which people compete with each other according to agreed rules **60**

gnawing (NAW ing) *v.* biting and cutting with teeth **47**

hesitated (HEZ i tayt id) *v.* stopped because of indecision **50**

identifiable (eye DEN tuh FY uh buhl) *adj.* recognizable; able to be identified **9, 31, 60**

infer (in FER) *v.* assume something based on facts **26**

injure (IN juhr) *v.* hurt someone or yourself **17, 27, 55**

instinctively (in STINGK tiv lee) *adv.* done automatically, without thinking **26, 52**

isolate (EYE suh LAYT) *v.* set apart from others; place alone **19, 27**

issue (ISH oo) *n.* problem or subject that people discuss **32**

liable (LY uh buhl) *adj.* likely to do something or to happen **53**

locate (LOH kayt) *v.* find the exact position of someone or something **27, 42**

lose (LOOZ) *v.* not win a game, argument, or war **69**

mauled (MAWLD) *v.* badly injured by biting and tearing **54**

monitor (MAHN i tuhr) *v.* carefully watch, listen to, or examine something over a period of time **28, 69**

negotiate (ni GOH shee ayt) *v.* discuss something in order to reach an agreement **26**

obtain (uhb TAYN) *v.* get something that you want, especially through your own effort, skill, or work **16, 61**

offensive (uh FEN siv) *adj.* unpleasant **28**

opposition (ahp uh ZISH uhn) *n.* strong disagreement with; protest against **32**

plead (PLEED) *v.* beg **55**

possible (PAHS uh buhl) *adj.* able to be done **14, 46, 61**

ravage (RAV ij) *v.* violently destroy; ruin **34**

refer (ri FER) *v.* look back **63**

reflecting (ri FLEKT ing) *v.* thinking seriously **64**

rely (ree LY) *v.* trust someone or something to do what you need or expect them to do **44, 59**

resolve (ri ZAHLV) *v.* find a satisfactory way of dealing with a problem or difficulty; settle **19, 26**

respond (ri SPAHND) *v.* react to something that has been said or done **17, 30, 52, 59**

restrict (ri STRIKT) *v.* keep within certain limits; put certain limitations on **46**

savoring (SAY vuhr ing) *v.* enjoying; tasting with delight **63**

seek (SEEK) *v.* try to find; search for; look for **17, 52**

speculate (SPEK yuh LAYT) *v.* make a prediction **67**

supervise (SOO puhr VYZ) *v.* oversee, direct, or manage work, workers, or a project **12**

support (suh POHRT) *v.* provide evidence for **60**

support (suh POHRT) *n.* evidence or reasons for **59**

survival (suhr VY vuhl) *n.* the state of continuing to live or exist **12**

survive (suhr VYV) *v.* continue to exist in spite of many difficulties and dangers **12, 25, 41**

systematically (sis tuh MAT ik lee) *adv.* orderly **33**

thrashing (THRASH ing) *adj.* wildly moving **27**

trace (TRAYS) *v.* follow the history of **73**

traversed (truh VERST) *v.* went across **42**

win (WIN) *v.* be the best or first in a competition, game, or election **69**

Photo Credits